The Lit1
of Woodland

by Rebecca Aburrow
Illustrations by Marion Lindsay

LITTLE BOOKS WITH BIG IDEAS

Featherstone Education
An imprint of Bloomsbury Publishing Plc

50 Bedford Square
London
WC1B 3DP
UK

1385 Broadway
New York
NY 10018
USA

www.bloomsbury.com

Bloomsbury is a registered trademark of Bloomsbury Publishing Plc

British Library Cataloguing-in-Publication Data
A catalogue record for this book is available from the British Library.

ISBN:
PB 978-1-4729-2137-6
ePDF 978-1-4729-2138-3

Library of Congress Cataloging-in-Publication Data
A catalog record for this book is available from the Library of Congress.

1 3 5 7 9 10 8 6 4 2

Printed and bound in India by Replika Press Pvt. Ltd

This book is produced using paper that is made from wood grown in managed,
sustainable forests. It is natural, renewable and recyclable. The logging and
manufacturing processes conform to the environmental regulations of the country of origin.

To view more of our titles please visit
www.bloomsbury.com

Contents

Introduction

'The best classroom and the richest cupboard is roofed only by the sky.
Margaret McMillan

Early years practitioners are fully aware of the importance and benefits of outdoor learning. In today's modern society, however, many children are not exposed enough to the natural world. The benefits of taking young children's outdoor learning to a woodland or leafy setting are endless: spending time in the calming environment of the woods contributes to lifelong learning and promotes a healthy lifestyle, and encourages children to become more active outdoors. It gives children the opportunity to observe the ever-changing systems of nature and dynamic world of plants and animals, and teaches them to respect and care for the environment and world in which they live.

Away from the restraint of their usual setting, children – in particular, kinaesthetic learners, children with SEN and children with EAL – thrive in a natural environment, and are likely to respond imaginatively and with curiosity to the outdoor world around them. The ideas in this book will help children to build their scientific knowledge and understanding of the natural world through play and exploration. The activities promote problem solving, critical thinking and help them to become confident risk takers, whilst also encouraging creativity and imaginative play.

Many early years practitioners are already witnessing the multiple benefits of outdoor learning in woodland settings by participating in 'Forest School' programmes. Forest School itself is very much a child-led initiative, that has the children's interests at the heart of its philosophy. This book can be used in conjunction with, and as a companion to, Forest School programmes, or can be used as a set of stand-alone activities for use in woodland or other natural settings. Every activity links to both prime and specific areas of the EYFS framework and can be simplified or made more challenging to suit the abilities of the children in your setting. Each one also offers ways of adapting the activity if you do not have access to woodland.

Links with the EYFS framework

The early learning goals that are particularly relevant to the activities in this book are as follows.

Prime Areas

Communication and language

1. Listening and attention: children listen attentively in a range of situations. They listen to stories, accurately anticipating key events and respond to what they hear with relevant comments, questions or actions. Children give their attention to what others say and respond appropriately, while engaged in another activity.

2. Understanding: children follow instructions involving several ideas or actions. They answer 'how' and 'why' questions about their experiences and in response to stories or events.

3. Speaking: children express themselves effectively, showing awareness of listeners needs. They use past, present and future forms accurately when talking about events that have happened or are to happen in the future. Children develop their own narratives and explanations by connecting ideas or events.

Physical development

1. Moving and handling: children show good control and co-ordination in large and small movements. They move confidently in a range of ways, safely negotiating space. Children handle equipment and tools effectively, including pencils for writing.

Personal, social and emotional development

1. Self-confidence and self-awareness: children are confident to try new activities, and say why they like some activities more than others. They are confident to speak in a familiar group, will talk about their ideas and will choose the resources they need for their chosen activities. Children say when they do or don't need help.

2. Managing feelings and behaviour: children work as part of a group or class and understand and follow the rules. They adjust their behaviour to different situations and take changes of routine in their stride.

3. Making relationships: children play co-operatively, taking turns with others. They take account of one another's ideas about how to organise their activity. Children show sensitivity to others' needs and feelings and form positive relationships with adults and other children.

Specific areas

Mathematics

1. Numbers: children count reliably with numbers 1 to 20, place them in order and say which number is one more or one less than a given number.

2. Shape, space and measures: children use everyday language to talk about size, weight, capacity, position, distance, time and money to compare quantities and objects and to solve problems. Children recognise, create and describe patterns. They explore characteristics of everyday objects and shapes and use mathematical language to describe them.

Understanding the world

1. The world: children know about similarities and differences in relation to places, objects, materials and living things. They talk about features of their own immediate environment and how environments vary from one another. Children make observations of animals and plants and explain why some things occur, and talk about changes.

2. Technology: children select and use technology for particular purposes.

Expressive arts and design

1. Exploring and using media and materials: children safely use and explore a variety of materials, tools and techniques, experimenting with colour, design, texture, form and function.

2. Being imaginative: children represent their own ideas, thoughts and feelings through design technology, art, music, dance, role play and stories.

Important things to consider

The site

You will need to think carefully about the site that you use. Consider whether you will take the children to public woods, or a park; alternatively, you could develop the grounds in your setting. There are many benefits when using public woods or parks: some areas are completely natural, and most offer a large space for children to explore, under your careful watch. However, you may need to ask your local council for permission to use the woods on a regular basis. You will also need to do a very careful site check before each visit (see 'site check', below). Consideration will need to be given as to how to best get to the site with your children.

Developing a 'natural' area in the grounds of your setting also has various benefits. Even the smallest of sites can be transformed to include exciting 'wild' areas, that are incredibly appealing for young children to explore. Planting shrubs and trees with the children is a great learning experience: it allows the children to take ownership of their outdoor learning area, and encourages them to care for it. Purchasing logs and bark will encourage wildlife to the area. Ask the children what they would like to see in their natural area and try to make this happen.

Site check

Each time you use the site, whether it is a public site or a site on your grounds, you must complete a site check. This must take place on three levels:

▶ Check the floor within and just outside the boundaries; check for sharp objects, trip hazards and animal faeces.

▶ Check at your eye level, and again at children's eye level, to ensure there are no sharp branches that could potentially hurt someone.

▶ Check at canopy level to make sure nothing is likely to fall and hurt someone.

Record any findings from the site check in a logbook, and remember to date and sign your assessment.

Correct clothing

It is important that you allow children to experience the woodland area in different types of weather (except high winds and storms). Children will need the correct clothing for every season.

Spring/Summer

▶ Summer hat

▶ Sun cream

▶ Layers of clothing

▶ Waterproof jackets

▶ Sensible shoes/wellies

Autumn/Winter

▶ Hats, gloves and scarves

▶ Warm clothing

▶ Waterproof jackets and trousers

▶ Wellies

Encourage the children to get themselves dressed and undressed before and after each session in the woods.

Kit bag

Each time you visit the woods you will need a kit bag/box of essential items. Suggested items include:

▶ First aid kit (at least one practitioner should be paediatric first aid trained, ideally with an outdoor element of qualification)

▶ Spare clothing for the children, depending on the season

▶ Water

▶ Health and Safety handbook (if your setting has one)

▶ Logbook (to record site checks)

▶ Mobile phone (in case of emergency)

▶ Toilet roll/tissues, nappy bags, toilet roll/baby wipes and hand sanitiser.

At the site

Boundaries

The boundaries of the site must be clearly established. This can be done using rope, ribbon or colourful pegs. It is useful to walk around the complete boundary with the children, especially the first few times they visit the area, so that they know how far they can roam.

Sharing circle

This is the circle where you, as practitioners, sit with the children to introduce activities and share ideas. The children can sit on logs or tree stumps, or alternatively on a large sheet of tarpaulin which can be laid on the floor during each session. You will need to have a signal to call the children to the circle: this could be ringing a bell, blowing a whistle or using a simple command.

Rules and responsibilities

Encourage the children to carry any equipment or resources needed to and from the site themselves, and to help each other on the way. Each time you visit the site, remind children of the rules. These can be rules that you devise together as a group (see 'Cherish our woodland' activity), but they should include some or all of the following:

▶ We enter the wood or forest respectfully

▶ We only collect fallen objects

▶ We do not put anything in or near our mouths

▶ We drag long/large sticks rather than trying to carry them

▶ We keep any smaller sticks we do carry by our sides

▶ We do not dig large holes

▶ We leave the site exactly as we found it

▶ We respect the site and each other.

Each activity identifies elements of both Enabling Environments and Positive Relationships, including specific vocabulary that can be introduced and modelled, alongside open-ended questions and enabling comments. Each experience includes:

▶ What to do if you don't have a woodland

▶ What you need;

▶ What you do;

▶ Taking it further.

Essential resources

Children need to have access to the following resources to successfully develop concepts about shape and space:

- ▶ Recycled materials to build with

- ▶ Commercially-produced construction equipment, both large and small, including small bricks, blocks and cubes

- ▶ Items to thread – plastic cotton reels, beads, natural objects, buttons

- ▶ Climbing equipment to explore

- ▶ Materials that changes shape – clay, play dough and plasticine

- ▶ Mark-making materials – chalk, paint, water and brushes, pencils, charcoal, sand, cornflour, mud, hypoallergenic shaving foam, finger paint

- ▶ Fruit and vegetables to explore e.g. at snack time and in cooking experiences

- ▶ Small world play resources

- ▶ Roadways, train tracks and materials to create pathways and routes

- ▶ A range of materials to create patterns with – shells, pebbles, conkers, fir cones, buttons, bangles

- ▶ Reference books and story books which explore aspects of shape and space

- ▶ Mirrors, mirror tiles, light box

- ▶ 2D shapes – plastic, card, wood

- ▶ Hollow and solid 3D shapes – plastic and wood

- ▶ Things to fill and empty – boxes, cylinders, some with removal lids

- ▶ Fabrics with repeating patterns

Size of group for activities

Some activities in this book suggest working with a group of a smaller size. This does not mean you cannot take a larger group of children with you to the woods; it simply means that the others can engage in free play for a time (observed by another practitioner), whilst you provide a focus group for a smaller number of children.

Technology

Even when you are spending time in the natural world, technology can still play an important role. Take photos and videos of the children during their activities – these are incredibly useful pieces of evidence for learning journals and observations, and are great to show parents. Plus the children will love watching themselves on screen back in the usual setting!

Cherish our woodland

This is a lovely simple activity that is best introduced during one of the children's first visits to the woods. It introduces the concept of the sustainability of the natural environment, at a very basic level. It teaches children about the importance of looking after and respecting the natural environment.

If you don't have woodland:
This is an activity that can easily be adapted to take place in any natural environment i.e. a park, garden, field etc.

Size of group:
This works well with a larger group of children.

What you need:

▶ Photograph of woodland

▶ Leaves (to be collected by children as part of the activity)

▶ Long, thin bamboo stick with a pointed end

▶ Wooden clothes pegs

What you do:

1. In your usual indoor setting, show the children a photo of woodland. Talk to them about the sorts of things they might see in the woods, the animals that might live there, and the sorts of rules we may need to have if we were to visit this area. Encourage them to think about caring for the plants, looking after and helping each other, and not disturbing the wildlife. This discussion will help when the children 'make promises' later in the woodland setting.

2. In the woodland, sit the children in a 'sharing circle' and insert the pointed end of the long bamboo stick into the ground, in the middle of the circle. Place a pile of clothes pegs next to the bamboo stick.

3. Tell the children that they will be searching for an interesting leaf in the woods today. Remind the children of the boundaries around the site and tell them that, when they have found their leaf, they must return to the sharing circle.

4. Let the children search the area for their leaf; then, after five minutes or so, signal for the children to return to the sharing circle if they have not already done so.

5. Ask the children to all hold their leaves in the air and encourage everyone to look around the circle at the different sorts of leaves that can be found in the woods. Explain that leaves have different sizes, shapes and colours and come from different types of trees.

6. Show the children a leaf that you have found and tell the children that this leaf is going to help them make a promise that must be kept whenever they visit the woods.

7. Model standing up, taking a peg from the pile and pegging your leaf to the bamboo stick in the middle. Say 'I promise I will never pick anything from something that is growing.'

8. Ask another practitioner to step forward and make another promise, e.g. 'I promise not to hurt anything that is living.'

9. Ask each child in turn to peg their leaf to the stick, making a promise if they can think of one. It does not matter if children repeat the same promises or even if they do not say anything at all – the activity can be repeated when they return to the woods, and they will be more than likely to think of new things to say in future visits.

10. When all the leaves have been pegged to the stick and all the 'promises' have been made, ask the children: 'How can we remember to keep these promises?' Suggest bringing the 'promise stick' with you each time you visit the woods, to remind the group what a special place it is.

11. End with the whole group repeating the following words after you: 'We promise to look after our planet and each other.' This might be something that you may like to say either at the beginning or at the end of each woodland session to emphasise the importance of caring for each other and the environment.

Taking it further:

▶ The 'promise stick' can be used for making rules back at the usual setting and is a great way of promoting communication and language. Encourage the children to listen to each other and remember the promises made by their friends as well as themselves.

My woodland treasure

This activity allows children to observe and value natural objects. It prompts them to find one natural object of interest, e.g. an acorn, conker or leaf, during their visit to the woods, and encourages speaking and listening whilst children describe their own and other's objects.

If you don't have woodland:

This is an activity that can easily be adapted to take place in any natural environment i.e. a park, garden, field etc.

Size of group:

This works well with a larger group of children.

What you need:

i will need

▶ A large treasure chest or a cardboard box covered in gold or silver shiny paper (the children can decorate this beforehand with jewels, shiny paper and glitter glue)

What you do:

1. In the usual setting, show the children the treasure chest and ask them what is usually found in a treasure chest. Explain that they are going to fill this chest with 'natural treasures'. Tell the children that they will each look for one special object in the woods to place in the treasure box.

2. Ask the children to sit very quietly in a circle in the woodland/leafy setting. Ask questions such as 'What can you hear?' 'What can you smell?' 'What can you see?'

3. Explain that the woods are a wonderful place where plants grow and many creatures live.

4. Tell the children that their challenge today is to find one small, special object that can be placed in the treasure chest. Encourage them to each choose a different item e.g. a conker, leaf, acorn, small piece of bark or a pebble.

5. Give the children the opportunity to wander around the woodland and observe the things around them. Remind them that they must not pass the string/tape boundary you have constructed. When they think they have found something special they can bring it back to the 'sharing circle'.

6. Place the treasure chest in the middle of the circle. As the children begin to return to the circle, ask them questions about their treasure and encourage them to show and talk about their objects.

7. The practitioner should choose an object of their own and hold it up. Model speaking a sentence about your item, e.g. 'This is my woodland treasure. It is very bumpy and rough.' Place the object into the treasure chest for all to see.

8. Ask each child to repeat the sentence starter: 'This is my woodland treasure. It is...' Describe their object and place it in the treasure box. Encourage adjectives such as 'round', 'green', 'spiky', 'slimy', 'hard', 'shiny' and 'crunchy'. Discuss some of the objects. Do the children know the name of each object and where it comes from?

Taking it further:

▶ Objects can be displayed in the treasure chest back in the usual setting. Each time the children visit the woods, they might like to look for other interesting objects that could be added to their collection.

Woodland bakery

Using paper cupcake cases and natural materials such as fallen flowers, leaves, nuts and seeds, children will create 'natural cupcakes' for Sid the squirrel. The activity will finish with them all joining in with singing an adapted version of 'Five Currant Buns in a Bakers Shop'.

If you don't have woodland:

The natural materials for the 'cupcakes' can be collected beforehand, and the activity then carried out in the normal setting.

Size of group:

This activity can be completed with the whole group of children.

What you need:

▶ Paper cupcake cases

▶ Large plastic spoons or scoops

▶ Picnic blanket or small folding table

▶ Squirrel puppet or soft toy (or large picture of a squirrel mounted on cardboard and stuck on a lollipop stick)

What you do:

1. In the woodland setting, sit the children in a sharing circle, with a small table or picnic blanket positioned in the middle.

2. Introduce the children to the puppet or toy, Sid the squirrel. Explain that squirrels collect acorns and other nuts and hide them in different places in the woods, ready for the winter. Take time to talk about squirrels and why they hoard acorns and other 'foods', and answer any questions the children might have.

3. Explain that Sid is upset because another animal has taken some of the acorns that he was storing for the winter. Tell the children that their challenge today is to surprise Sid the squirrel and create some 'natural cupcakes' that he might like.

4. Give each child a spoon and a paper cupcake case. Show them how to place a spoonful of mud into the paper case first. Remind them not to fill the case too full as the paper might break.

5. Ask the children what 'squirrel food' they could use that Sid might like, such as nuts, acorns, bits of plant etc. Remind the children that the cakes are not suitable for children to eat.

6. The children should begin collecting items to add to their cupcake cases, then should return to the circle to make their 'natural cupcakes'. When the cupcakes have been made, the children should place them on the middle of the table.

7. The children can then call for Sid to come back and look at his surprise. When he does not appear, suggest that a song is sung to entice him out.

8. Suggest singing the following song to the tune of 'Five Currant Buns'.

9. Place five cakes at the front of the table or the edge of the blanket and begin to sing:

> Five cupcakes in a woodland shop,
>
> Round and fat with acorns on top.
>
> Along came Sid the Squirrel one day,
>
> Bought a cupcake and took it away.

10. Sid should 'appear' and take a cake away. Ask the children to join with you in the singing until Sid has taken all five of the cupcakes.

11. Ask the children what they think Sid will do with the cupcakes. Explain to the children that squirrels store food for the winter and that he might like to hide the cupcakes away until wintertime.

12. Depending on time available, practitioners might like to introduce the children to the game 'Hide an acorn' (see page 33).

Taking it further:

▶ Back in the setting, ask the children to explain back to you why Sidney was hiding food. Show them a video clip or a photograph of squirrels hiding acorns and nuts ready for the winter. Encourage the children to draw pictures of squirrels. Ask them to think of other creatures or objects in the woods that begin with the letter 's'.

Who lives in a house like this?

In this activity, children will discover where different woodland creatures live. Nests, hollows, holes and burrows are pointed out and children must decide who or what could live there!

If you don't have woodland:

This activity will work best in woodland, as the woods provide a lot more scope for finding animals' homes; however, it can be completed in any outdoor setting in which children can turn over rocks, look in trees and streams and peer underneath bushes.

Size of group:

Begin with a smaller group of around six children.

What you need:

▶ Camera

▶ Laminated photographs of woodland animals and birds e.g. barn owl, wood mouse, butterfly, squirrel, frog, wren

▶ Laminated photographs of various places each creature could live e.g. a tree hollow or the rafters of a disused building, an underground nest in a burrow, the underside of a leaf in a hedgerow, the branches of a tree, a pond or under a plant, and a nest in a bush, nook or cranny!

What you do:

1. Prior to visiting the woodland, show the children a variety of photographs of creatures that can be found in the woods (see list of examples above).

2. Ask the children if they know any of the creatures' names. Ask them where they think each of the creatures could be seen. Explain that all of these creatures can live in the woodland but that we may not always see them, as it may be the wrong season (too hot or too cold), or the wrong time of day. Explain that some animals are nocturnal, which means they sleep during the day; barn owls are mostly nocturnal, and wood mice almost entirely.

3. Now show the children some of the 'animal home' pictures. Ask questions such as: 'Which creature do you think might live in the pond?' 'Which creature do you think might live in a nest?'

4. Place all of the picture cards on the floor, evenly spaced out, and ask the children if they can match the 'animal cards' with the 'home cards'. It does not matter if they do not match the cards correctly – this is simply an exercise to get the children talking and the vocabulary flowing. Encourage vocabulary such as 'nest', 'pond', 'tree', 'hollow', 'bush' etc. and the names for each of the animals.

5. When the activity is complete, discuss with the children why they made their choices. Ask questions such as: 'Why would it be hard for a vole to live in a nest that is high up in a tree?' or 'Why would the butterfly not live in the pond?'

6. Explain to the children that when they visit the woods they are going to try and find some of animal homes. If they spot any of the homes, they can take a picture with the camera.

7. In the woodland setting, remind the children what their task for today is. Show them the animal photographs and see if they can remember the names of the creatures.

8. Tell the children to sit down and close their eyes whilst you (or another practitioner) place each animal card in a place where the animal might live, e.g. a frog near a puddle, a butterfly in a bush, a squirrel in a tree, etc.

9. Ask the children to open their eyes and stand up. Tell them that they should try to find the picture of each animal near the place that animal might live. When the children find the animal card, they must move it to another location in the wood where the animal could also live.

10. When each animal has been found and 're-homed', walk around with the group of children looking at the animals' new homes. For each animal, talk about whether the home chosen was a good choice.

Taking it further:

▶ Repeat the activity at a later date using fictional characters from stories or fairies, witches and trolls. A picture of each character can be placed next to puddles, near logs, in hollows of trees, etc. This provides a good opportunity for developing children's speaking and listening skills, as they can discuss where each character might like to live and why.

Time for tree

This action game teaches children that many trees are deciduous, and allows them to observe the changes that occur in this type of tree throughout the seasons.

If you don't have woodland:

This activity can take place anywhere that has a variety of deciduous and evergreen trees. It works best in autumn and winter.

Size of group:

One large group of children.

What you need:

▶ A setting that has a variety of evergreen and deciduous trees

What you do:

1. Ask the children to walk around and look at the different trees in the woods. Show the children an evergreen tree. Explain that this type of tree keeps its green leaves all year round – even in the autumn and winter.

2. Show the children a tree that loses its leaves. Ask them to tell you what is different about this tree. Explain that in autumn, the green leaves change colour and fall from the branches. Tell the children that in winter, these sorts of trees have bare branches because all of the leaves have fallen off.

3. Explain to the children that you are going to play an action game to help remind them what happens to some trees in each of the four seasons. Tell them that they are going to 'become' trees! Show the children the actions required for each season.

   Spring: Arms and legs slightly apart (to indicate the growth of the leaves)

   Summer: Arms and legs wide apart (to indicate a full bushy tree)

   Autumn: Wiggle fingers through the air (to indicate leaves falling from the trees)

   Winter: Shivering action (to indicate bare branches)

4. When each season is called out, the children must all do the actions. Children who do not complete the correct action have to sit out.

5. To begin with, the practitioner should call out each season, but later in the game a child might like to take on this role.

6. Each time you visit the woods/trees, encourage the children to observe the changes that have taken place. Photograph the same deciduous tree at various points in the year so that the children can see how different it looks in each season.

Taking it further:

▶ Back in the usual setting, provide each child with a piece of paper divided into four equal sections. In each section there should be a line drawing of a bare tree. Children can finger print different coloured paint on three of the trees; for example, pink paint as blossom for Spring, green paint for Summer, red and yellow for Autumn, and the tree left bare for Winter.

▶ Each time you visit the woods/trees, encourage the children to observe the changes that take place, sometimes from one week to another. Photograph the same deciduous tree at various points in the year so the children can see how different it looks in each season.

Texture treasure hunt

This is a great opportunity for using and listening to descriptive language. Children are given the task of finding objects of different textures: something rough, something smooth, something slimy... the variations are endless! A 'feely box' can be created for later discussions.

If you don't have woodland:

This activity can be completed anywhere outdoors using the local environment.

Size of group:

This activity works better with smaller groups of about 4-6 children, but can be completed with the whole group.

What you need:

▶ A large box for collecting items, or treasure chest (previously decorated by the children)

What you do:

1. In the woodland setting, sit the children in the sharing circle and explain that today's woodland challenge is a treasure hunt.

2. Tell the children that they will be given a clue for each item that needs to be found. Explain that the object they are looking for will be small enough to fit in their hand.

3. Come up with a 'signal' that instructs the children to come back to the sharing circle – this could be a whistle, a horn, a call, etc. Make sure the signal can be heard from the furthest perimeter point.

4. Give the children their first clue: 'Find something smooth.' Before sending the children off to look for something smooth, remind them that when they hear the signal they must return to the sharing circle, even if they haven't found their object.

5. When each child has returned to the sharing circle, look at some of the objects they have found. Ask questions such as: 'Are all the objects smooth?' 'Do the objects feel smooth all over?' 'Can anyone think of any other words to describe them?' 'What colours are they?' Ask the children to vote for their three favourite textured objects, and then place them in the treasure box/chest.

6. Next, send the children to find something rough, repeating the activity. Ideas for further variations include something slimy, something dry and something wet.

Taking it further:

▶ Children can give their own suggestions of what to collect next; this will encourage descriptive vocabulary. The treasure chest can be taken back to the usual setting and its treasures displayed accordingly!

Splashes of colour

This is an activity that can be repeated at various times throughout the year. It encourages children to become more observant of the ever-changing systems of nature that take place across the seasons, and provides an opportunity for them to use technology in a natural setting.

If you don't have woodland:

This activity can be completed in a number of ways. If natural objects of various colours are available in the school grounds, they can be photographed; the activity can also be carried out using man-made objects found in and around the children's usual setting.

Size of group:

Smaller groups of around 6 children per practitioner are ideal.

What you need:

▶ A digital camera or tablet for photographing objects, or a bag in which to collect objects

▶ A photograph of woodland

What you do:

1. In the usual setting, show the children a typical photograph of the woods. Ask them to tell you what they can see in the picture. Encourage vocabulary such as 'trees', 'leaves', 'bushes', 'branches' etc.

2. Invite the children to name the colours that they can see in the picture. Young children are likely to say that they can see the colour green, and possibly the colour brown. Encourage them to look more closely and see if they can spot any other colours.

3. Tell the children that their challenge is to find as many different colours as they can in the woods, and to take a photograph of each colour. If no cameras or tablets are available then a plastic bag to collect fallen objects will work just as well.

4. In the woodland setting, sit the children in a circle and explain that you would like them to find a natural object that is yellow. At this point, it is useful to remind children what a natural object is and explain that they must not pick anything that is growing. It is useful for the practitioner to be aware of colours that could be seen at various points in the year and to choose their colours accordingly.

5. As a group, search for something yellow. When an item has been found, demonstrate taking a picture that is 'close up'. Explain that the screen needs to show as much of that colour as possible.

6. Continue searching, and make sure that each child in the group gets a turn at taking a photograph of something yellow. When the children have taken their photographs, return to the circle and compare the photographs (or objects) collected. Is each photo of something natural? If necessary, remind the children of the difference between natural and man-made objects. Repeat the procedure for as many colours as are visible in the woods.

7. In the usual setting, upload the photos to the IWB and show them to the rest of the group. Children can be invited to sort and group the pictures (this can be by shape and size of object, as well as colour) – teach them how to drag and drop on the large screen. If you decide to collect objects instead of taking photographs, the objects can be attached to a display board or placed on a display table, and again the children can sort them into colours, shapes and sizes.

Taking it further:

▶ Use the photos or objects to create a montage of colour, in the form of a rainbow. You could also create a man-made rainbow montage, using objects around the children's usual setting. This will provide opportunities to discuss different sorts of materials and their names.

Minibeast patrol

Support children in correctly identifying various bugs on a picture sheet, then challenge them to find the minibeasts in the woodland by gently turning over rocks, examining leaves and looking in the hollows of trees!

If you don't have woodland:

This activity can also be completed in the setting's garden or outside area, or in the local park.

Size of group:

This can include the whole group.

What you need:

▶ A pre-prepared worksheet showing simple pictures of four easily identifiable creatures likely to be found in the woodland setting, e.g. woodlouse, spider, caterpillar and ant.

▶ Clipboards

▶ Pencils

▶ Pictures of minibeasts – either in a book, from the internet or on a poster

▶ Digital camera or tablet (if available)

What you do:

1. At the children's usual setting, explain that today's woodland challenge is to become 'minibeast seekers'! Explain that 'seek' is another word for 'look for', and that the mission is to look for four different types of minibeast.

2. Ask the children if they have seen a spider before. Ask: 'What does a spider look like?' 'How many legs does a spider have?' Show the children a picture of a spider and talk about it. Ask if anyone knows where spiders live. You could also talk about how spiders spin webs, and explain that the children might see some spider webs today if they look carefully.

3. Repeat the procedure with each of the four minibeasts on the worksheet you prepared earlier.

4. Show the children the worksheet. Explain that each time they spot one of these minibeasts they need to put a mark next to the picture. Demonstrate how to do this.

5. In the woodland setting, sit the children in a circle. Ask if they can remember the names of the creatures that they will be looking for today.

6. Tell the children that they must be very careful not to hurt any of the animals and not to damage or destroy any of their homes. Explain that many creatures can often be found under logs or rocks. Show the children how to carefully lift a log or stone and look underneath. Demonstrate placing the stone or log gently back down again. If possible, show the children the hollow of a tree and explain that creatures may also be seen here.

7. Tell the children that if they spot a really interesting creature they can take a photograph of it.

8. When the children have had time to explore, ask them to return to the sharing circle. Invite the children to share what they have found by modelling: 'The most interesting thing I found today was a spider. The spider had caught a fly in his web.' Ask each child to repeat the phrase 'The most interesting thing I found today was...'

9. Ask the children to compare tick sheets. Ask: 'Did anyone find any other creatures?' 'What do you think they were?'

Taking it further:

▶ Look at the data collected. Ask the children questions: 'How many spiders did we see?', 'How many caterpillars did we see?' etc. Ask the children to each choose their favourite minibeast from the four. Make a human graph by asking the children to stand in one of four lines: those who like spiders best, those who like caterpillars best, etc. Take a photograph of the children from above. Show the children the photograph either by printing it out or by showing it on the interactive whiteboard. Look at the line of children that like spiders. How many children like spiders? Which is the longest line? Which is the most popular creature? Which is the shortest line?

Leaftastic

In this activity, children observe the leaves that grow on different types of trees. They are given the opportunity to collect leaves, count them, sort them into shapes, colours and sizes, and create leaf pictures and collages.

If you don't have woodland:

This activity can also be completed in the setting's garden or outside area, or the local park. Children can also collect leaves at home or on their way to school, or practitioners can take children on a local walk where they are likely to see a variety of trees.

Size of group:

This can include the whole group.

What you need:

▶ Bags for collecting leaves

▶ Large plastic trays for sorting leaves

What you do:

1. In the woodland setting, sit the children in a circle and tell them to look around at the trees. Do they all look the same? Depending on the time of year, do they all have leaves? What colour are the leaves? If they are green, are they the same shade of green?

2. Explain that there are many types of trees, and each has different shaped and different coloured leaves. Remind them of the activity 'Time for tree', in which the children learned that some trees keep their leaves all year round, while other trees have leaves that change colour and fall in the autumn. Tell the children they should collect as many different leaves as possible and place them in their bags.

3. Give the children a little while to find different leaves on the ground and put them in their bags.

4. Call the children back to the circle and ask them to take one leaf from their bag and hold it up. Tell all the children to look around the circle and observe how each leaf is different.

5. Upon return to the usual setting, share all the leaves between five or six plastic trays. Tell the children that, as a group, you would like to sort the leaves. Ask them to firstly sort the leaves into size. Can they order the leaves in size? Then move onto colours. Ask the children what colours of leaves they found. Can they place the leaves into piles of each colour? More able children may be also want to sort the leaves into shapes.

Taking it further:

▶ Ask the children to create a leaf picture by sticking the leaves onto a piece of card. You may wish to draw the outline of a tree on each piece of card, so that children can stick the leaves within the outline. More able children may want to try creating a repeating pattern picture using a selection of different leaves.

Hide an acorn

This activity allows children to learn about animals that store food, such as squirrels. It introduces them to a game where they must 'hide and seek' acorns; the activity can be adapted to focus on other types of seed depending on the time of year.

If you don't have woodland:
This activity works better in a woodland setting, but can be completed in any outdoor area.

Size of group:
At least 12 children.

What you need:

▶ A picture or video clip of a squirrel hoarding acorns

▶ A bag of acorns (or other seasonal seeds)

What you do:

1. In the usual setting, show the children a picture of a squirrel. Ask them if they know what this animal is called. Point out his long, bushy tail, beady eyes and pointed ears. Ask the children if they know where squirrels live.

2. Explain to the children that squirrels live in the woods and are well known for hoarding acorns and other nuts. Show the children an acorn, and explain that acorns come from oak trees. Ask the children if they know why squirrels collect lots of acorns and hide them away. If possible, show the children a video clip or a picture of a squirrel gathering and hoarding acorns.

3. In the woodland setting, sit the children in the 'sharing circle'. Ask them if they can remember what squirrels like to collect. If it is the right time of year, ask the children to collect their own acorns for the game; if not, you can produce a bag of acorns or alternate seeds/nuts.

4. Explain to the children that they are going to pretend to be squirrels who are hoarding their acorns. Tell them that sometimes squirrels also take the acorns that have been hidden by other squirrels!

5. Teach the children the following rhyme and practise singing it through together.

   (To the tune of 'I'm a Little Teapot'):

   > I'm a little squirrel
   > Fast as can be,
   > I am hoarding
   > Acorns for my tea.
   > If I find some,
   > I will smile,
   > And take them back
   > To my own pile.

6. Choose two children to sit in the middle of the sharing circle.

7. Give the other children two or three acorns each to place behind them, around the outside of the circle. Do not let them position the acorns too far away from the circle – a couple of paces at most. When the acorns have been placed, ask the children to sit back down in the circle.

8. The two children from the middle should walk around the outside of the circle, trying to find as many of the acorns as possible; the other children must chant the rhyme twice through (or listen as the practitioners chant the rhyme, and join in when they are ready).

9. Once the rhyme has been chanted twice, ask the children to bring the acorns they have found back to the middle of the circle. Encourage the children to count how many acorns each 'seeking' child found, and ask questions such as 'Which 'squirrel' found the most?' 'How many more acorns did one squirrel find than the other?' 'Can you count how many acorns were found altogether?'

10. Tell the children to retrieve any acorns that were not found, and to return to the circle.

11. The child who found the most acorns can choose the next two children to sit in the middle and find the acorns.

Taking it further:

▶ Take the acorns back to the usual setting and encourage the children to paint the smooth parts of the acorns in different colours. Display the coloured acorns in a large glass or clear plastic jar. Alternatively, remove the acorns' 'hats' and stick them on thick card to create three dimensional acorn artwork.

A nest for the owl babies

This activity allows children to observe that birds make nests, and gives them the opportunity to create their own! This task will encourage children's mathematical and scientific vocabulary and increase their knowledge and understanding of the world, as well as drawing upon their imaginations!

If you don't have woodland:

Practitioners and children could bring in a collection of natural objects from home in order to complete the activity in the usual setting. Alternatively, it can be carried out in a local park or any area where trees are present.

Size of group:

This activity is suitable for the whole group of children, but it will work better if it is completed in small groups.

What you need:

▶ A copy of *Owl Babies* by Martin Waddell

▶ Plastic/cloth bags or cardboard boxes

What you do:

1. In their usual setting, show the children a copy of the book *Owl Babies*. Ask them which birds are on the front cover of the book. Do the children know anything about owls? Explain that owls are nocturnal, which means that they sleep in the day and are awake at night-time.

2. Read the story to the children. Talk about the illustrations and discuss the feelings of the owls at various points in the story. Pause at the part of the story where the three owl babies sit on the branch together.

3. Explain to the children that it is sometimes hard when we have to leave our parents, but we know they will come back. (Be sensitive to any children whose parents are separated, or if a child has suffered a parental bereavement.) Prompt a discussion about a time when the children have felt sad or lonely. Ask if they have any ideas about how we could help cheer up the owls.

4. Explain to the children that when they get to the woods today, their challenge will be to create a new nest for Sarah, Percy and Bill, which will help them to feel warm and safe when their mum goes hunting.

5. At the woodland/leafy setting, remind the children what their woodland challenge is. Can the children spot any nests in any of the trees? What sorts of materials do birds use to make nests? Look around the woods together for suitable natural materials before the children embark on collecting anything.

6. Sit the children down in the sharing circle and give each small group a bag or box in which to collect their items, and then allow them to start collecting!

7. Upon the children's return to the circle, encourage them to use any larger items at the bottom of their nest. Ask them what shape their nest should be. Encourage them to think of ways to keep the materials together.

8. Try to get the children to talk to each other as much as possible. It is not a problem if their nest falls apart: this is a great activity for encouraging speaking, listening and problem solving, so if the nest falls apart, ask: 'How can it be fixed?' 'What will hold it together?'

9. Praise each group for something they have done well, e.g. 'This group were good at collecting lots of different materials.' 'This group were very helpful to each other.' 'This group listened carefully to each other's ideas.'

Taking it further:

▶ Take some natural materials back to the usual setting. Make a group collage of the three owls from the story sitting in a nest, using a combination of natural and man-made materials.

A hotel fit for a minibeast

In this activity, children will build a minibeast hotel using natural and environmentally friendly materials. Over the following weeks, they can observe the hotel to see how many insects come to stay!

If you don't have woodland:

This activity can be completed in any natural setting where leaves, twigs, bark, pebbles and stones are available.

Size of group:

This activity works in pairs, or in small groups of 3-4 children.

What you need:

▶ Wooden crates or wooden boxes that can easily be stacked

▶ Ceramic bricks or ceramic pots

▶ Cardboard tubes

▶ Natural items found in woods

What you do:

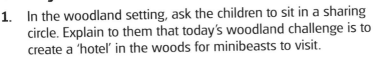

1. In the woodland setting, ask the children to sit in a sharing circle. Explain to them that today's woodland challenge is to create a 'hotel' in the woods for minibeasts to visit.

2. Show the children one of the wooden crates or boxes and demonstrate how they can stack on top of each other. Explain that this will allow room for lots of creatures. Ask the children which creatures they think may visit this hotel.

3. Show the children how the ceramic pots and cardboard tubes can be inserted between the wooden crates.

4. Ask the children to hunt for other natural, fallen items in the woods that could be used to build the hotel.

5. Ask the children to begin constructing their hotel using the man-made and natural materials. Remind the children that there needs to be areas in the hotel where the minibeasts can hide and feel warm and safe.

6. As the children are building their hotel, talk to them about the shapes, textures and colours of the items they are using. Ask them to think about what each room could contain, and how the minibeasts could use it – for instance, they may wish to include a room for the bugs to exercise in, with items to climb over, under and around.

7. When the minibeast hotel is complete, ask the children to predict who they think will be the first minibeast guests at the hotel!

Taking it further:

▶ Return to the woods the following week and ask the children to peep inside the hotel. They can gently turn over items and objects to see if there are any minibeasts underneath. Can they tell you the names of the minibeasts that they have found? The hotel can be observed during each visit to the woods. A class tally chart or pictogram of minibeasts spotted can be displayed in the usual setting.

Woodland creatures

In this activity, the children use their imaginations and transform a ball of plasticine into a woodland creature of their choice, using only natural materials.

If you don't have woodland:

This activity works better in a woodland setting, but can also take place outdoors in a local park or other leafy area.

Size of group:

This activity can be carried out with any number of children.

What you need:

▶ Pictures of woodland creatures (ideally mounted on card and laminated) e.g. hedgehog, squirrel, spider, mole

▶ Small balls of plasticine or other malleable material, the size of a child's clenched fist (one per child).

What you do:

1. In the woodland setting, sit the children in the sharing circle. Ask them if they spotted any woodland creatures on the way to the woods today, and whether they can see any creatures now. Ask them if they know the names of some of the creatures that live in the woods.

2. After some suggestions, show the children the pictures you have prepared. Hold up the first picture, e.g. hedgehog, and ask the children if they know what the creature is called and whether they can tell you something about this creature. Look at the hedgehog's features: what is special about him? Explain that a hedgehog's 'spikes' are called 'spines'. Repeat this procedure with each of your chosen woodland animals.

3. Now show the children the ball of plasticine and ask them to create a woodland creature using only this ball of plasticine and natural, fallen materials from around the wood. Remind the children of the boundary lines before sending them to collect natural objects.

4. Demonstrate how to insert small twigs, leaves and tiny stones into the plasticine.

5. Whilst the children are creating their 'creatures', it will be interesting to note if any of them change the shape of the plasticine to accommodate the body shape of their chosen creature.

6. Sound the signal for everyone to return to the 'sharing circle'. Ask various children to show their creature to the rest of the group. Encourage the other children to take turns to ask questions about each creature and to guess what their friends have made.

Taking it further:

▶ Create a table display featuring all of the woodland creatures made by the children. The display could contain speech bubbles recording things the children have said when describing their own, and their friends', creatures.

A boat for Little Ant

This activity introduces children to materials that float and sink. Their challenge is to create a boat from materials that they find in the woods, that will successfully carry Little Ant across a puddle (or stream)!

If you don't have woodland:

This activity requires a variety of natural materials that children can use to make their 'boat', but it can be completed in the usual setting if these materials are collected beforehand. If a large puddle, stream or pond is unavailable then a large builder's tray full of water can be used.

Size of group:

The children will need to be in smaller groups of 4-6 to complete this activity.

What you need:

▶ Natural items found in woods (a bag of natural items if completing at the usual setting)

▶ A large puddle/stream (or tray to put water in)

▶ A laminated photograph of an ant

What you do:

1. In the woodland setting, sit the children in a circle and show them a photograph of an ant. Tell them that Little Ant wants to visit his friend who lives on the other side of the puddle (or stream).

2. Ask the children for suggestions of ways that Little Ant could cross the puddle. Explain that most ants can't swim – so how else could he cross?

3. Wait until a child suggests 'a boat', or prompt the children until they give this answer. Tell them that they are going to make a little boat that could carry ant over the stream.

4. Take the children to the water source. Show them a natural object, such as a piece of bark. Ask them what they think will happen to the bark when it is put in the water. Tell them that if the object stays on top of the water, it 'floats'. If it drops to the bottom of the water, it 'sinks'.

5. Demonstrate how some objects sink and some float by dropping them into the water. Ask the children to predict the result before each object is dropped in the water, using the vocabulary 'float' and 'sink'.

6. Ask the children to choose some fallen natural objects that they think will float and use them to make a little boat for Little Ant. If they would like to join materials together, they can.

7. Give the children time to choose their materials and create their boats, then give the signal to indicate that it is time for them to return to the water source to test their boats.

8. Take each of their boats and place them, one by one, onto the water. Give each boat a gentle nudge: ask the children which boat travels the furthest and floats the best. Talk about the materials that were used. Which materials were the best floating materials? Which materials sank?

Taking it further:

▶ In the usual setting, ask the children to find five objects that float and five objects that sink, by testing the various objects and materials in a large water tray.

A natural orchestra

In this activity, children can make a variety of homemade musical instruments from natural materials.

If you don't have woodland:

Children can collect a variety of natural objects from outside the setting, or can bring some materials in from home with which they can make their instruments.

Size of group:

This activity works well with at least 10 children.

What you need:

▶ A variety of natural materials

▶ Small cardboard boxes

▶ Plastic tubes and bottles

What you do:

1. Ask the children to sit in a sharing circle. Explain that the children are going to try making as many different sounds as possible, using only items found in the wood.

2. Show the children a handful of dry leaves (depending on the time of year) and demonstrate how they make a 'crackling, rustling' sound. You could also take two sticks and tap them together, and ask the children to listen to the noise that the sticks make.

3. Ask the children to each find something in the wood that makes an interesting sound. When they have found their item, they need to bring it back to the sharing circle.

4. After ten minutes has passed, signal for the remaining children to return to the circle. Ask all the children to hold their natural items up high for everyone to see.

5. Explain that when you tap each child on the shoulder, they need to make a sound using the item that they found.

6. Ask the children if they thought any of the sounds sounded like musical instruments. If so, which instruments did they sound like?

7. Show the children the collection of boxes, bottles and tubes. Can they use these to make their natural items into a musical instrument? Demonstrate by placing the crisp leaves into a box and shaking it.

8. Give the children time to create their 'musical instruments', and then signal for them all to return to the sharing circle.

9. Choose a favourite song or nursery rhyme to sing, and ask the children to accompany the song by playing their natural musical instruments.

Taking it further:

► Children can use their instruments to create different sounds for each season of the year. For example, spring could be represented by the tinkling of a handful of tiny stones or shells, as plants start to grow and birds start to sing.

We're going on a teddy bear hunt!

This is an opportunity for children to 'show good control and coordination in large movements' and to 'move confidently in a range of ways' (EYFS Profile 2014). The children will follow a natural obstacle course whilst re-enacting Michael Rosen's well loved story *We're Going on a Bear Hunt*. A teddy bear will be hidden at the end of the course for the children to find.

If you don't have woodland:
This activity can be completed in any space outdoors. If natural obstacles are unavailable, use man-made obstacles such as long fabric tunnels, stepping stones, mats, sandpits and more!

Size of group:
Smaller groups of up to 6 children will work better for this activity.

What you need:

▶ *We're Going on a Bear Hunt* by Michael Rosen

▶ A pre-determined route through the woods that includes a variety of natural objects, e.g. shallow streams, fallen trees, large tree stumps, long grass etc.

▶ Wellies and waterproof clothing

▶ A digital camera

▶ A teddy bear (hidden at the end of the obstacle course)

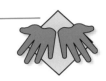

What you do:

1. Before starting the activity with the children, plan your route through the wood, making sure you will encounter various natural obstacles on the way.

2. Read the children the story *We're Going on a Bear Hunt.*

3. Invite the children to chant with you as you read the chorus on each page:

    We're going on a bear hunt

    We're going to catch a big one.

    What a beautiful day!

    We're not scared.

4. Discuss the story with the children. Where were the children going? What happened on the way? What did the children have to go through?

5. Tell the children that they are going to go on a 'teddy bear hunt' through the woods.

6. In the woods, ask another practitioner to hide the teddy bear at the end of your route. Make sure the children are wearing their wellies and waterproof clothing. Explain to them that in order to start the teddy bear hunt, they need to begin by walking around the sharing circle, chanting the chorus in step 3 together.

7. When the children have mastered the chant, begin to walk around the route previously set out. Keep chanting until you reach the first obstacle e.g. the stream.

8. Ask: 'What noises do you think we will hear as we walk through the stream?' Encourage onomatopoeic words and phrases such as 'splish-splash' and 'drip-drop'. Walk through the stream together, repeating the words. Photograph the children at each obstacle (the photographs can be used for sequencing activities upon return to the usual setting).

9. When each child has waded through the stream, walk on, chanting the rhyme until you reach the second obstacle e.g. long grass. Again, ask the children what noises they might make as they walk through the grass; then walk through the grass together, repeating the words e.g. 'swish, swoosh'.

10. After the final obstacle, tell the children that the teddy bear is hiding somewhere close by and that they must find him.

11. After you have completed the whole route and the children have found the teddy bear, you may wish to hide the teddy bear in a new position and start again at the beginning – this time seeing if the children can remember the words each time they encounter an obstacle.

Taking it further:

▶ Print out the photographs of each 'obstacle', or else show them on the interactive whiteboard. Use the photographs to help the children retell the story together, following the correct sequence. Encourage the children to recall the words and actions they used at each obstacle as each photograph is revealed.

Welly walk

This is a great activity to incorporate learning about phonics. Children will love the excitement of wearing their wellies to walk through the woods, puddles, streams and mud! This woodland challenge encourages them to describe what they see, hear and smell on their journey.

If you don't have woodland:

This activity works especially well if there are water sources or muddy areas available. If you are not using woodland, it would be useful to prepare a route beforehand. If possible, incorporate the street environment as well as the natural so that the differences can be spotted.

Size of group:

A smaller group of 6-8 children with each practitioner works best for this activity; however, it can also be carried out with larger groups of children.

What you need:

▶ A selection of pictures of 'things found in the woods' and 'things not found in the woods' e.g. post box, shop, car, tree, log

▶ Fishing nets

What you do:

1. In their usual setting, tell the children that they will be wearing their wellies and going for an interesting walk today. Give each child a fishing net and explain to them that this is to 'catch' sounds and smells on the way!

2. Begin your walk. Allow the children to walk a little way, then ask them to stop and stand very still. Ask: 'What can you hear?'

3. Tell them to choose a sound and 'catch' it in their net so that they can save it for later: this will prompt the children to really focus on the different sounds around them.

4. Now ask the children what they can smell or feel. Encourage them to also catch scents and feelings in their nets.

5. In the woods, encourage the children to walk through streams, mud, mossy areas etc. Stop every so often and ask them to tell you what they can see, smell and hear. The children should 'catch' each of these things in their fishing nets. Every so often, ask them to stop and reach out to touch different objects, for instance, a slimy rock, a rough piece of bark, a shiny leaf etc. Encourage them to use as many adjectives as possible to describe the textures.

6. Next, ask the children to find objects that begin with specific sounds of your choice, possibly linked to phonics taught that day or week. How may objects can they find?

7. At the end of the welly walk, sit the children in the sharing circle and ask them to reach into their nets and 'pull out' a sound they heard today. Ask where this sound was heard and what was making the sound. Now ask them to reach into their nets and pull out a smell. Ask questions like 'Is it a nice smell?' 'Where did you smell this smell?'

8. Talk to the children about their feelings during the walk. How did their feelings change during the welly walk, if at all? Did the sounds and smells change?

Taking it further:

▶ In the usual setting, gather a series of pictures of objects seen on your walk. Ask the children to sort the pictures into 'Things found in the woods' and 'Things not found in the woods'.

This is not a stick

This singing game allows children to 'explore and use media and materials' (EYFS Profile 2014) using their imaginations. When they sing the magic song, their stick is transformed into an object of their choice – from fairy wand to pirate sword, to a paddle for a boat or a witch's broom!

If you don't have woodland:

This activity can be completed in the usual setting; simply collect the sticks beforehand.

Size of group:

One large group of children.

What you need:

▶ Sticks – one per child.

What you do:

1. In the woodland setting, ask the children to sit in the sharing circle. Tell them that there is some magic in the air today, and that if they learn the magical song, very magical things will happen!

2. Explain to the children that in order for the magic to work, they must each find a stick. Remind children about safety when carrying sticks and inform them that the magic will not work for anyone who waves their stick in the air.

3. When the children return to the circle, tell them that they need to tap some magic into their sticks. Tap a simple rhythm with your stick on the floor in front of you, and encourage the children to repeat the rhythm. Tap another rhythm and repeat the procedure. You could invite a child to also tap a rhythm for the group to repeat.

4. Now tell the children that if they all learn the following magical song, each of their sticks will transform into something different. To the tune of 'The Farmer in the Dell', begin to sing:

   This is not a stick

   This is not a stick

   Magic, magic

   This is not a stick!

6. As a group, sing the song a few times over, then step into the middle of the circle and say: 'Wow! This is not a stick! It's an oar for my rowing boat – I'm going to row down the stream today!' Act out rowing with your stick.

7. Explain to the children that they can make their sticks magically turn into something different by chanting the song. If necessary, repeat the demonstration, this time changing your stick to a pirate sword/fairy wand/witch's broomstick.

8. Each time the song is sung, choose a child to step into the circle and transform their stick. It might be necessary for practitioners to question and prompt some children into explaining what their stick is and what it does.

Taking it further:

▶ Take sticks back to the usual setting and paint and decorate them according to the objects the children spoke about. Display the decorated sticks and label them. You may also wish to read *Stick Man* by Julia Donaldson with the children, and discuss all the ways in which stick man is used in the story.

Is there room on the broom?

This uses the popular story *Room on the Broom* by Julia Donaldson, and allows children to respond imaginatively whilst re-enacting the story using simple dramatic techniques. They will love devising a 'woodland spell' to conjure up a brand new broomstick for the witch to use!

If you don't have woodland:
This activity can be completed in any outdoor setting.

Size of group:
This activity can be completed with as few as 6 children, or as many as the whole group.

What you need:

▶ A copy of *Room on the Broom* by Julia Donaldson

▶ A large pot or a container that can be used as a cauldron

What you do:

1. Read the children the story *Room on the Broom*.
   Talk about the story, the characters, the woods and the weather.

2. In the woodland setting, sit the children in the sharing circle and show them the storybook again. Ask them if they can remember what happens in the story. Tell the children that they are going to help you read the story by joining in with certain parts. Ask them to join in with actions to the following parts of the story (practise the actions several times with the children):

   'Down!' cried the witch

   (Children to swoop to the ground)

   And they flew to the ground

   (Arms outstretched in a flying motion)

   They searched for the ....

   (Looking all around the area)

   But no .... could be found.

   (Puzzled looks on faces, arms outstretched with palms to sky.)

3. Read the story and encourage the children to join in with the actions.

4. Stop reading towards the end of the story when the witch 'fills up her cauldron'. Ask the children which natural items they could use to fill the cauldron and create a spell.

5. Model placing the first item in the cauldron, e.g. two petals, and say the words: 'I am going to add two soft silky petals to the cauldron.'

6. Tell the children that the spell only works if they describe their item, thus encouraging them to use adjectives. Encourage the children to think about how their object looks, smells, feels, etc.

7.   Ask the children to each find something in the woods that they would like to use for the spell. Encourage them to come forward and place his/her item in the cauldron, remembering to describe it.

8.   When all of the items have been placed in the cauldron, ask the children to recite the spell below. Hold hands and walk around in a circle, chanting:

Iggity Ziggity Zaggity Zoom

Iggity Ziggity Zaggity Zoom

Out rose a truly magnificent broom!

9.   At this point, hand the children their imaginary brooms. Encourage them to 'fly' on their brooms around the area.

Taking it further:

▶   Ask the children to describe what they saw whilst flying on their brooms. Encourage them to use vocabulary relating to the woodland/outdoor area in which the activity takes place.

Phonics in nature

This activity develops and reinforces children's phonic knowledge, and can be linked to particular sounds that the practitioner wishes to develop.

If you don't have woodland:

This activity can be completed in any natural outdoor setting.

Size of group:

This activity is suitable for the whole group.

What you need:

▶ Collecting bags or baskets
▶ Camera or tablet (optional)
▶ Large stick, suitable for marking out a letter in the mud

I will need

What you do:

1. Find a muddy area in the woodland/natural setting. Explain to the children that you are going to make a mark in the mud and you would like them to work out what sound the mark on the ground makes. This can be linked to phonics the children are learning that week or any phonics that need reinforcing.

2. Form a letter in the muddy ground e.g. the letter 'p'. If the letter is not clearly visible, the practitioner can show flash cards or create the letter from natural materials. Ask the children: 'What sound does this letter make?'

3. The children must then search around for something beginning with 'p' and bring it back to the sharing circle when they hear the signal. Photograph the object if it is too large to collect. Remind the children only to collect fallen items.

4. Look at all the objects that have been found, and ask the children to say the names of the items together. Ask questions such as: 'Do they all start with the same sound?' 'If not, which sounds do they start with?' 'Is there a 'p' sound anywhere else in the word?'

5. Repeat the procedure by creating a new letter in the mud. More able children can try to write letters in the mud or create letters from natural objects.

6. End the activity by asking each child to find a natural object that starts with the same sound as the first letter of their name.

Taking it further:

▶ Take some natural objects back to the usual setting. Create a display of natural objects beginning with the same sounds.

The woodland wizard

This game teaches children to think about the movements, actions and sounds of woodland animals using physical drama.

If you don't have woodland:

Playing this game in the woodland setting can add to the fun, but it is not necessary. This game works equally as well played in an open space in the children's usual setting.

Size of group:

The game can include the whole group.

What you need:

▶ A magician's wand (or stick found in the woods!)

▶ A tambourine (or equivalent musical instrument)

▶ An interactive whiteboard on which to watch video clips, or a large board to pin pictures to

▶ Short video clips (or images) of around six different woodland animals e.g. hedgehog, bird, squirrel, mole

What you do:

1. In the usual setting, begin by showing the children a video clip (or image) of one of the woodland animals, e.g. a mole. Ask: 'How is the mole moving?' 'Slowly or quickly?' 'What is he doing with his paws?'

2. Ask the children to stand up and make their hands into 'mole paws'. Ask: 'How did the mole's paws move?' 'What else was the mole doing?' Challenge the children to try and move around as moles.

3. Explain to the children that whenever they hear the tambourine they must 'freeze'.

4. Shake the tambourine and repeat the activity using some of the other animals as inspiration. Encourage the children to look at how quickly the animals move, how they move their limbs, what sort of facial expressions they have, and whether they are likely to be carrying anything in their paws or beaks.

5. In the woodland setting, ask the children if they can remember some of the animals that might be found there. Have the children spotted any of these animals today? If so, which ones?

6. Tell the children that the woodland wizard's magic wand will turn them into different animals. The wizard will decide which child was the 'best animal'. Remind the children that each time they hear the tambourine they must 'freeze', and they must help sing the magic song to make the magic work:

   Woodland animals everywhere!

   How do they move?

   Let's all share!

7. After the rhyme, the woodland wizard waves the wand and shouts out the animal. All the children must change the shape of their bodies and move in the manner of the chosen animal.

8. Let the children move for a count of ten seconds, and then shake the tambourine. Ask the child who demonstrated the best movements to show the others, then allow them to become the wizard and choose the next animal for the children to enact.

Taking it further:

▶ Ask the children to think about the sounds that these animals make.

We've got the whole world in our hands

This activity allows children to create a plaster cast of their own footprints and handprints, and encourages them to look for the tracks of other animals. It is important to remember to check children's hands for any cuts before allowing them to dip their hands in mud. You should also ensure that children wash their hands thoroughly when they return to the usual setting.

If you don't have woodland:

Children's footprints and handprints can be created in the same way in the usual setting.

Size of group:

A small group of around 4 children.

What you need:

▶ Plaster of Paris

▶ Large mixing bowl

- Bottle of water
- Strips of card (about 5cm wide), taped or glued at either end to create a circle
- Stick
- Trowel

What you do:

1. Explain to the children that wherever any animal goes, they leave tracks behind them. Ask the children to look around them. Can they spot any footprints that have been made today? Ask: 'Do the footprints stay in the mud forever?' 'When do the footprints disappear?'

2. Tell the children that they are going to make a muddy handprint, and that they are going to keep this handprint by making a 'cast' of it. Explain that a 'cast' is a hard piece of plaster.

3. Together with the children, find a muddy area suitable for working in. Smooth the area with a flat stick and show the children how to press one their hands firmly into the mud.

4. Take the circular piece of card and press it firmly around the handprint.

5. Pour about a cup of water into the bowl, then carefully sprinkle the plaster into the water. Keep pouring until the plaster forms a little mountain with the peak above the water surface.

6. Slowly mix the water and plaster until the mixture is thick and creamy.

7. Gently tap the bowl on the hard ground to remove any air bubbles.

8. Pour the mixture slowly into the side of the print on the ground and let it seep into the middle to fill the print. Fill to the top of the cardboard circle.

9. Leave the cast harden for about 30 minutes, then using the small trowel dig around the area, including the mud.

10. Wrap the whole thing in newspaper as it is still very fragile. It will remain fragile for a couple of days.

Taking it further:

- Encourage the children to look for animal tracks on the wet ground and in the mud. Look near water sources such as river banks, streams, rivers and ponds. Create casts of each print and try to identify the animal that made the tracks.

Mud detectives

In this fun game, children will develop their mark making abilities by using sticks to make simple marks, letters, numbers and names in the mud.

If you don't have woodland:
A large muddy or sandy area and some long sticks are all you need to carry out this activity.

Size of group:
Smaller groups work better.

What you need:

▶ A large area of mud/wet sand

▶ Some long sticks

What you do:

1. In the woodland setting, tell the children that they are going to become 'mud detectives'! Explain that a detective is a sort of policeman or policewoman who solves problems. In order to be a 'mud detective', they will first need to find a stick that is about as long as their legs!

2. Once all the children have found a stick, ask them to return to the sharing circle and place their sticks on the floor in front of them.

3. Tell the children that playing 'mud detectives' can be great fun, but it can also be dangerous if the sticks are not played with safely. Tell them that if anyone waves their stick in the air the chief detective (practitioner!) will remove it from them.

4. Lead the way to the large area of mud. Explain to the children that they can practise making marks in the mud with their sticks. They can make clues by trying to mark their name, a number or a letter.

5. When the children have had sufficient practice, ask them to gather around. The children must close their eyes while you (the chief detective) writes the first clue. Once you are ready, the children should open their eyes and identify what letter or number you have made.

6. The child who identifies the letter/number/word (or even shape) correctly must then make a mark in the mud, and the game continues.

Taking it further:

▶ In the usual setting, continue the game by making marks, shapes, letters, numbers or names with large paintbrushes and a bucket of water on walls or concrete flooring.

Woodland counting

This is a perfect opportunity to bring mathematical learning to the woodland setting. Children are asked to count from 1 to 20 and place the numbers in order, adding the correct number of natural objects to each card.

If you don't have woodland:
This activity can be completed outside in the children's usual setting and can be carried out using both natural and man-made objects.

Size of group:
The game can include the whole group, but works better with smaller groups of children.

What you need:

▶ Several sets of large A3 or A2 (laminated) cards, each with a number between 0 and 20 written on the top half of the card. The bottom half of the card should be left blank.

What you do:

1. In the woodland setting, sit the children in the sharing circle and explain that today's woodland challenge involves counting and searching for objects.

2. Explain to the children that some of the woodland animals don't understand numbers and so we are going to try and help them to understand. Show them the pack of jumbled number cards.

3. Give each small group of children a pack of cards and ask them to place them in order on the floor in a line. Ensure the children are spread out and have plenty of space, so that their numbers do not overlap.

4. Check each group have placed the numbers in the correct order, and correct any misconceptions.

5. Hold up one number card, e.g. number 4. Explain to the children that they now have to find four objects to place on this card. Find four items, e.g. four twigs, and show the children how to place the twigs on the bottom half of the number card.

6. Ask the children to complete each number card in the same way – finding the corresponding number of natural items to match each of the numerals.

7. When completed, take photographs of each 'natural number line'.

Taking it further:

▶ Hold up one number card and ask the children who can be the first to find 'one more' object than the number held (i.e. if you are holding the number 3, they must find 4 objects). This can be repeated several times. Then try again, but this time they must find the number of objects 'one less' than the number that you are holding.

Natural shape spotting

This fun activity will develop children's understanding of shape and improve their recall of the names and properties of different shapes.

If you don't have woodland:
This activity can be completed anywhere outdoors using the local environment.

Size of group:
This activity is suitable for the whole group.

What you need:

▶ Four large plastic shapes (e.g. circle, square, triangle, rectangle)

▶ A cloth bag

What you do:

1. In the woodland setting, explain to the children that they will be playing a game to do with shapes.

2. Tell the children that in order to play the game, they need to remember the names of four shapes. Ask one child to come and choose a shape from your bag. Ask them to hold it up for everyone to see. Ask the whole group if they know what shape it is. Repeat this activity for each of the four shapes.

3. Now take one shape, e.g. a circle, and hold it up for everyone to see. Tell the children that you would like them to find a circle in the woods today. Can they find an object that looks like a circle or some objects that together make a circle in the woods?

4. Send the children to look around the woodland to see if they can find a circle. If the object is small enough, they can bring it back to the sharing circle. If they decide to make a circle from several larger objects, go over to view the shape.

5. Repeat the activity for each of the four shapes, encouraging the children to count the number of sides that each shape has.

6. The children can then be encouraged to create large-scale versions of each of the shapes using natural materials such as twigs and leaves.

Taking it further:

▶ Offer the children the opportunity to take photographs of the natural objects they find that create various shapes. These photographs can be uploaded to the interactive whiteboard for the children to sort into groups; alternatively, they can be printed off and then displayed after sorting.

Perfect patterns

This activity focuses on repeating patterns. The practitioner will demonstrate a repeating pattern using natural items, and the children will then be encouraged to complete the pattern.

26

If you don't have woodland:

This activity will work in any outdoor area that has sufficient natural resources, e.g. twigs, small stones and fallen leaves.

Size of group:

This activity works better with smaller groups of 6-8 children.

What you need:

▶ Collecting bags or baskets

▶ Camera

I will need

What you do:

1. In the woodland setting, ask the children to sit in the sharing circle and explain to them that they will be playing a game based on patterns. To begin the game, they need to collect certain objects and bring them back to the circle.

2. First, show the children a small twig and explain that they have five minutes to collect as many small twigs in their bags/baskets as they can. Remind them that when they hear the signal they must return to the sharing circle.

3. Allow the children sufficient time to collect the twigs, then raise the signal for them to return to the sharing circle. Ask them to count how many twigs they found. Ask questions such as: 'Who found the most twigs?' 'Who found the least twigs?' 'Did anyone find the same number of twigs as another person?' 'Who found the longest twig?' 'Who found the shortest twig?'

4. Ask the children to place all of their twigs in a pile in the middle of the sharing circle.

5. Now repeat the activity with small stones, then fallen flowers, fallen leaves, etc.

6. When an adequate amount of each natural material has been collected, explain to the children that you are all going to use the materials to make a pattern.

7. Begin by placing a twig on the floor, then put down a small stone next to it, followed by another twig and then another small stone. Invite the children one by one to place the next object. If an object is placed incorrectly then a new pattern must be started.

8. When the children are confident with a two-object repeating pattern, increase to three objects or more. Each time an object is placed incorrectly, start a new pattern.

9. When the children are confident with this game, ask them if they can make patterns of their own.

10. Record the children's patterns by taking photographs. You could also record what they say about their patterns, either by noting it down or using a camcorder to video them.

Taking it further:

▶ Take some natural objects back to the usual setting. Can the children use the objects to create another pattern? Stick/attach their patterns to thick card and display them alongside the photographs that were taken.

Bundles of sticks

This activity provides an excellent opportunity for children to develop their mathematical skills, and to practise mathematical vocabulary such as 'long', 'short', 'longer', 'shorter', 'light', 'heavy', 'lighter', 'heavier', 'count', 'order' and 'sort'. The activity ends with the children making a trail of sticks and estimating how far the line will reach.

If you don't have woodland:
This activity can be completed in any area where sticks are available. This can include the setting's grounds or in a local park.

Size of group:
A smaller group of around 6 children will work better for this activity.

What you need:

▶ The children will collect their own sticks for this activity

What you do:

1. In the woodland setting, ask the children to sit in a sharing circle and explain that in the woods we can find many interesting sticks that have fallen from trees.

2. Ask the children to each look for a stick in the woods. Remind the children that the stick must have already fallen from the tree, and that we should never pull or snap sticks from trees.

3. When the children hear the signal, they must return to the sharing circle with their stick. Remind them to carry their sticks by their sides when they walk.

4. Back in the circle, ask each child to place their stick on their lap, or on the floor in front of them. Ask questions that will develop their measuring skills, such as 'Whose stick is the longest?'

5. Now line the sticks up next to each other and compare them. Look at the differences between them. Encourage vocabulary such as 'long', 'longer', 'longest', 'short', 'shorter', 'shortest', 'thick', 'thin' etc.

6. Can the children line the sticks up in size order? Ask them which stick they think is the heaviest and why. Which do they think is the lightest and why? How can they tell? Show the children how to place a stick in each hand, and explain that the stick that pulls their hand down the most is the heaviest.

7. Complete the activity by lining the sticks up in a row, end to end, to see how far the line of sticks will stretch. Ask the children to estimate the distance. Ask questions such as 'Do you think they will reach that tree?'

Taking it further:

▶ Collect all the sticks together and play a game of 'stick towers'. Put all the sticks into a pile; in turn, children must try to pull a stick out from the pile without disrupting the others.

Super natural heroes

In this activity, children are given the opportunity to create their own superhero capes from natural materials, and play a superhero game in a natural setting.

If you don't have woodland:

This activity will work in any outdoor area that has sufficient natural resources, e.g. fallen leaves, petals and seeds. Alternatively, collect these beforehand and carry out the activity in the usual setting.

Size of group:

This activity can be done with as few as 6 children or as many as the whole class.

What you need:

▶ Pre-cut capes made from crêpe paper or thin fabric, each with a length of ribbon attached to the top

▶ Sticky-back plastic

▶ Superhero toy, or a cardboard cut-out of a superhero

▶ Superhero masks (optional)

What you do:

1. Sit the children in a circle in the woodland setting.

2. Introduce the superhero toy or cardboard cut-out. Explain this is Captain Treetop and he is a superhero. The only problem is that Captain Treetop keeps getting lost in the woods and only a 'natural' superhero is able to find him!

3. Ask the children if they would like to become natural superheroes for the day. Explain that in order to do this they will need to make a special superhero cape.

4. Show the children one of the pre-cut capes (you only need to bring one with you to the wood). Explain that they need to collect small objects from the wood, which they are going to stick to their capes when they return to the usual setting.

5. Show the children a variety of natural objects, e.g. leaves, stems, acorns, seeds etc. You may wish to recap on basic vocabulary e.g. 'bark', 'leaf', 'stem', 'flower', 'acorn' etc. This could be particularly useful for EAL learners.

6. Encourage the children to feel the objects and introduce other vocabulary such as 'rough', 'smooth', 'heavy', 'light', 'natural' and 'man-made'. Ask: Why would heavy materials be unsuitable? Why would rough materials be unsuitable? Decide with the children which natural materials would be suitable for sticking on the capes.

7. Ask the children to collect some items that will be suitable for sticking on their capes, and to bring the items back to the sharing circle.

8. Take all the collected items back to the usual setting, then support the children in sticking them to the pre-cut capes. When all the capes are dry and the items are firmly in place, cover each cape with sticky-back plastic. Then let the children put on their capes and become natural superheroes!

Taking it further:

▶ Ask the children to sit in a circle whilst wearing their capes. Ask them what natural superheroes might do. Model flying into the circle wearing a cape. Say: 'My name is Superhero .... (your name) and I like helping animals!' Encourage the children, one by one, to fly into the circle and complete the sentence 'My name is Superhero .... and I ....'.

Muddy prints

Children will love the experience of putting their bare hands in squelchy, slimy mud! This activity allows them to explore the different textures of dry soil and wet mud. Remember to check the children's hands for any cuts before allowing them to dip their hands in mud, and remind children to rinse their hands thoroughly with soap and water and wash thoroughly again upon returning to the usual setting.

If you don't have woodland:
This activity can be completed anywhere that mud can be found!

Size of group:
This activity is suitable for the whole group.

What you need:

▶ Large rolls of thick backing paper or wallpaper

▶ Soap, water and antibacterial hand gel

What you do:

1. In the woodland setting, ask the children to sit in the sharing circle and explain to them that they are going to create a piece of mud art using only their hands.

2. On the ground, roll out a small piece of thick paper and weigh it down with large stones.

3. Pour some water on the ground (if not already muddy and wet), and demonstrate what happens to dry soil when water is poured on it. Place the palm of your hand into the mud, ensuring the mud covers your whole hand.

4. Show the children how to create a muddy handprint by placing your hand flat onto the paper. Ask the children how they think the mud feels on their skin.

5. Roll out another larger section of paper for the children to print on. After each child has made a muddy print, write their initials below the handprint. As the children dip their hands in the mud, talk about how it feels. Ask questions like 'Is it warm or cold?' 'Is it thick?' 'What sounds are made when we sink our hands into the mud?' 'Is it oozy and squelchy?'

6. Ask the children: 'What happens to the mud as it dries on your hand?' Encourage the children to realise that it dries because their hands are warm; the mud becomes lighter in colour and flakes away.

Taking it further:

▶ Upon return to the usual setting, encourage the children to use scissors to carefully cut out their handprints. The handprints could be used to create a class picture of a winter tree, with the hands and fingers acting as the tree's branches.

▶ Add googly eyes or feathers to handprints to make mud monsters or mud creatures!

▶ Use small circular pieces of wood on which to print the 'muddy hands'. The circles of wood can be hung somewhere in the setting.

A lovely leaf

This activity introduces children to the different types of trees that can be found in woodland or parkland. It demonstrates that not all trees are the same; they all look different and have different leaves, bark and seeds. The children will be able to take a leaf of their choice back to the usual setting and use it to create a leaf mobile, or a stained glass window.

If you don't have woodland:
This activity can be carried out in any setting that has several different trees.

Size of group:
The whole group can complete this activity, but it might be advisable to complete the art activity in smaller groups back in the usual setting.

What you need:

▶ A variety of leaves (ideally different shapes and colours)

▶ Squares of coloured tissue paper (enough to cover a large leaf with a border around the outside)

▶ PVA glue

▶ Coat hanger, or a washing line and pegs

What you do:

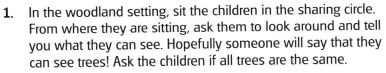

1. In the woodland setting, sit the children in the sharing circle. From where they are sitting, ask them to look around and tell you what they can see. Hopefully someone will say that they can see trees! Ask the children if all trees are the same.

2. Explain that trees are very large plants, and that all plants are similar but not the same. Different types of trees have different leaves, bark, flowers, seeds and fruit, and are called different names.

3. Ask the children to walk around the wood and pick up some fallen leaves. Tell them to bring the leaves back to the sharing circle and place them in the middle. After five minutes, signal to all the children that they must return to the sharing circle.

4. When all the children have returned, show them some examples of different leaves. It is not necessary to name the trees that the leaves have come from; at this stage, the children simply need to be made aware that there are different types of trees. Encourage the children to discuss the different shapes and to name the colours.

5. Now ask the children to each hunt for one special leaf. Encourage them to find a leaf that is not torn or damp if possible. The children will use their special leaf to make a piece of art later.

6. Signal for all children to return to the sharing circle. Show them the leaf that you have chosen. Hold the leaf up and repeat the following words, inserting an appropriate adjective to describe your leaf:

   My leaf is ....

   As you can see;

   My leaf is lovely, to me.

7. Encourage the children to follow your model, each choosing a word to describe their leaf.

8. Back in the usual setting, ask each child to place his or her leaf in the centre of a piece of coloured tissue paper and to drizzle PVA glue over the leaf and tissue paper.

9. Next, tell them to place a second piece of tissue paper over the top and gently press down around the leaf. Ask the children how the leaf looks and feels now; they may respond with words such as 'soggy', 'wrinkly' or 'colourful'.

10. Once dry, each leaf can be cut out and threaded with string or ribbon, and then hung from a class washing line, a coat hanger or similar. As the light catches the leaves, the PVA glue will make the leaves shine and they will flutter gently in a breeze.

Taking it further:

▶ Use the leaves to create a montage, which can then be stuck to the window to create a stained glass window effect. Children can also complete this activity with fallen flowers, flat seeds and other similar items.

The **Little Books** series consists of:

50
All through the year
Bags, Boxes & Trays
Big Projects
Bricks & Boxes
Celebrations
Christmas
Circle Time
Clay and Malleable Materials
Clothes and Fabric
Colour, Shape and Number
Cooking from Stories
Cooking Together
Counting
Dance
Dens
Discovery Bottles
Dough
Drama from Stories
Explorations
Fine Motor Skills
Free and Found
Fun on a Shoestring
Games with Sounds
Gross Motor Skills
Growing Things
Investigations
Junk Music
Kitchen Stuff
Language Fun
Light and Shadow

Listening
Living Things
Look and Listen
Making Books and Cards
Making Poetry
Maps and Plans
Mark Making
Maths Activities
Maths from Stories
Maths Outdoors
Maths Problem Solving
Maths Songs and Games
Messy Play
Minibeast Hotels
Multi-sensory Stories
Music
Music and Movement
Numbers
Nursery Rhymes
Opposites
Outdoor Play
Outside in All Weathers
Painting
Parachute Play
Persona Dolls
Phonics
Playground Games
Print Making
Prop Boxes for Role Play
Props for Writing
Puppet Making

Puppets in Stories
Resistant Materials
Rhythm and Raps
Role Play
Role Play Windows
Sand and Water
Science through Art
Scissor Skills
Seasons
Sequencing Skills
Sewing and Weaving
Shape and Space
Small World Play
Sound Ideas
Special Days
Stories from around the world
Story bags
Storyboards
Storybuilding
Storytelling
Time and Money
Time and Place
Topsy Turvy
Traditional Tales
Treasure Baskets
Treasure Boxes
Tuff Spot Activities
Washing lines
Woodwork
Writing

All available from
www.bloomsbury.com/featherstone

The Little Books Club

There is always something in Little Books to help and inspire you.
Packed full of lovely ideas, Little Books meet the need for exciting and
practical activities that are fun to do, address the Early Learning Goals
and can be followed in most settings. Everyone is a winner!

We publish 5 new Little Books a year. Little Books Club members receive
each of these 5 books as soon as they are published for a reduced price.
The subscription cost is £29.99 – a one off payment that buys
the 5 new books for £4.99 instead of £8.99 each.

In addition to this, Little Books Club Members receive:
· Free postage and packing on anything ordered from the
  Featherstone catalogue
· A 15% discount voucher upon joining which can be used to buy any
  number of books from the Featherstone catalogue
· Members price of £4.99 on any additional Little Book purchased
· A regular, free newsletter dealing with club news, special offers and
  aspects of Early Years curriculum and practice
· All new Little Books on approval - return in good condition within 30
  days and we'll refund the cost to your club account

Call 020 7458 0200 or email: littlebooks@bloomsbury.com for
an enrolment pack. Or download an application form from our website:

www.bloomsbury.com